NEW SOUTHERN HOUSES

American Houses Today

The New Native House: Towards an Integral Architecture

Scott L. Guyon, Architect

NEW SOUTHERN HOUSES

American Houses Today

The New Native House: Towards an Integral Architecture

Scott L. Guyon, Architect

Copyright © 2004 by:
GUYON ARCHITECTS, INC.
401 WEST MAIN STREET, SUITE 333
LEXINGTON, KENTUCKY 40507

Packaged by:
GRAYSON PUBLISHING
JAMES G. TRULOVE, PUBLISHER
1250 28TH STREET NW
WASHINGTON, DC 20007
202-337-1380
JTRULOVE@AOL.COM

Design:
JAMES PITTMAN

First published in 2004 by:
WATSON-GUPTILL PUBLICATIONS,
A DIVISION OF VNU BUSINESS MEDIA INC.,
770 BROADWAY, NEW YORK, NY 10003
WWW.WATSONGUPTILL.COM

Library of Congress Control Number: 2004109166

ISBN: 0-8230-3184-5

Manufactured in Korea
First Printing, 2004

1 2 3 4 5 6 7 8 9 / 07 06 05 04

Dedication

Special thanks and recognition to my chief collaborator architect, Paul Swisher.

My heartfelt thanks to Clyde Carpenter, a truly brilliant teacher of architecture.

This book celebrates my partnership and devotion to Chesney and our children Hunter and Coleman. It is truly their support and inspiration which makes my life possible.

Contents

What is 'New Native'

1. *The use of:* **'Folk' house—forms as inspiration (Essence)**
2. *The use of:* **Local context (Soul)**
3. *The use of:* **International Modern Architecture (Intellect)**
4. *The use of:* **Natural Materials (Body)**
5. *The use of:* **Balancing Opposite Forces (Spirit)**
6. *The use of:* **Mindful Budgets (Society)**

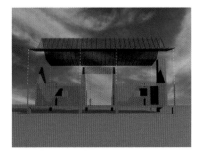

(Top Left) Photo of Dogtrot folk house

(Above Left) Computer rendering revealing slot of open space

(Top Right) Plan of dogtrot house

(Above Right) Computer rendering of dogtrot house

'FOLK' HOUSE—FORMS AS INSPIRATION (Essence)

In an age of electronic hyperbole and information overload the 'folk' forms found in the handmade houses and barns of the south seem to possess a clear and halting essence. The plain houses and "work" buildings of the American South are simple, direct and beautiful. Every region of the world possesses these "native" structures. Their powerful ideas are found in all later elite forms of architecture. It is their essence that gives rise to the modern house I call New Native.

When the design process begins in my office the plan-forms that float in and out of the early sketches of my houses include the venerable dogtrot, the saddlebag and the double-pen. Also present are the shotgun, the I-house, the two-door tenant house and the old central passage. The essential quality of these "right-angle" plans can sometimes remind me of the chord changes of I, IV, &V found at the epicenter of much of American blues music; close to the ground and always relevant. Despite their "3-chord" geometry, these little folk buildings provide an endless source of variation for my early drawings.

It may be that poverty and the scarcity of materials caused an accidental simplicity in these vernacular houses but when I look at them more closely there seems to an intangible quality of 'knowing' by the builders. It is as if their sense of the landscape or the act of walking to and from the site seems to have informed the basic intelligence of these structures. The 'New Native' as I develop it today is actually liberated by the reference to these early rudimentary buildings in the way that any limit or rule can trigger new responses and new inventions. It is the lack of formal complexity that sets the stage for unpredictable richness as the design evolves.

Dogtrot

Of all the folk house types it is probably the *dogtrot* that is the most well known. It is the *dogtrot* that evokes the classic scene of the handmade house with its "tin roof" and its see-through porch. Its most compelling elements are its single sheltering roof and its "slot" of open space that runs from the front to the back of the plan.

The *dogtrot* is a clear example of the basic architectural device known as solid and void. The two volumes that make up the kitchen on one side and the sleeping area on the other are left with an open space between them. This is called the *dogtrot*. It sets a dramatic visual effect in which one can see the daylit landscape while at the same time viewing the covered slot and adjacent porches in shadow. This combination of deep shadows and the brightness of the "framed" landscape is a wonderful and satisfying experience.

The *dogtrot* plan was a simple response to climate and materials. The "breathing" spaces found around the closed rooms provided ventilation and porch space for the occupants. The *dogtrot* form has provided a beginning for many of the New Native projects. The centered slot and the punctuation of open space and closed volumes can be seen in this collection at the Lisa-Noel, Burgess Smith and Coughlin Residences.

The *dogtrot* itself sets up a basic arrangement often found in modern design; the floating roof with free elements arranged below.

Saddlebag

The *saddlebag* house has attached to its name the myth and legend of equine culture in general and the cowboy saddlebag in particular. The *saddlebag* name develops from the appearance in the house of a major chimney, centrally located, with a roof attached to either side of its mass. Hence, the chimney is the "horse" and the "saddle-bags" are the rooms that seem to be hung from it.

The saddlebag plan is used in the New Native to designate the hearth or chimney as the "center" and is often the beginning of the design. The chimney is added onto while also providing a primary division between the spaces.

The charm and mystery of chimneys as gathering places to take refuge around is present in the *saddlebag* type as it anchors each house to the ground. The chimney can then start to act as the main support for the stair or other central elements like powder rooms and special closets.

The New Native plan, influenced by the *saddlebag,* can then be seen as those spaces "north" and "south" of the fireplace. Further significance is given by marking public spaces (living rooms, kitchens, etc.) to one side of the chimney and private spaces (sleeping rooms, reading rooms, etc.) to the other.

In this way the original *saddlebag* form can generate the arrangement of basic spaces and simultaneously evoke the memories of "hearth and home" associated with rural life.

Despite their "3-chord" geometry, these little folk buildings provide an endless source of variation for my early drawings.

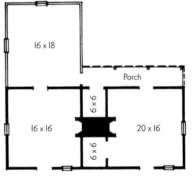

(Top Left) Photo of Saddlebag folk house

(Above Left) Computer rendering of Saddlebag house

(Top Right) Plan of Saddlebag

(Above Right) Computer rendering revealing the anchoring chimney

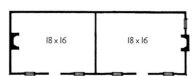

(Top Left) Photo of Double Pen folk house

(Above Left) Computer rendering of Double Pen

(Top Right) Plan of Double Pen

(Above Right) Computer rendering revealing spilt program

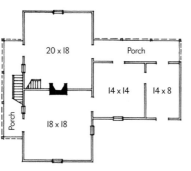

(Top Left) Photo of traditional I-House

(Above Left) Computer rendering of I-House

(Top Right) Plan of I-House

(Above Right) Computer rendering revealing flanking space around a central corridor

Double-pen

The *double-pen* house consists of a basic arrangement of one rectangular volume placed immediately beside another. The front doors announce the way in and the way out. The hallway for this house is outside often across a simple front porch.

In its utter simplicity, the *double-pen* embodies our most primary impulse toward making shelter. The two "pens" are quickly placed on the ground and the activities between the two rooms are assigned for sleeping on one side and living and cooking on the other. It is in this folk house form that the possibility of repetition is first discovered. Of course the poetic suggestions of "twins" or "doubles" can be folded in with this repetition thus yielding an expanding set of intriguing plans and elevations.

Traces and influences of these "side by side" rooms can be found throughout the New Native series. It is critical to understand this plan, as with the others (dogtrot, saddle bag, etc.) as reinterpreted rather than directly copied. The Jackson-Vance house has, for example, two identical "halves" along the front of the main elevation but it is not literally divided by a single inside wall, as you would find in the original double-pen layout.

As another example, the Coughlin house contains a repeating space on either side of a center living room and can be said to double itself from left to right in a manner at least suggestive of the old *double-pen* type.

The *double-pen* offers a chance to express the obvious; the same figure twice. Further, it speaks directly to the straight forward construction of just two rooms. As if to say, two rooms are enough! So the *double-pen* contributes to the New Native house as a reminder of the power of repetition and the unexpected richness of doubling of any one thing.

I-house

The *I-house* is the most physically elaborate structure to influence the New Native with its vertical shape and centralized arrangement of spaces. So named by Fred Kniffen in the 1930's not because it is formed like the letter "I," but rather because this house type is found so often in Indiana, Illinois and Iowa. It is the frontier-American equivalent of the New England "center hall" colonial.

The plan is strikingly simple; stairs in the center beyond the front door with a single room to the right and a single room to the left. Because the body of the house was typically only one room deep, the end elevations are pleasingly vertical and well proportioned. While the *I-house* plan is essentially very simple its variations were many. Ells, porches and additions did occur and in this way the New Native house will also step out here and there to reinterpret the basic central plan.

The Meier house is an example of a strongly centered house, which refers to the "I" in several ways. There is a familiar centered front door with two flanking rooms but then an exception is taken with the location of the stair to the left edge of the plan. Rather than the central stair as an object of interest the fireplace is expanded and placed as the "stand-in" for the formal main stair. As another example, the Taylor residence is influenced by the "I" type. It borrows its central stair location from the central foyer of the *I-house* entry and leads the visitor to a view of the garden beyond.

The "I" plan is used in the New Native to spur on the possibility of the community space. The central hall of the "I" plan is inspirational in creating open spaces where people may convene and engage one another. A special moment may be found as one is greeted in the center hall or it may express itself as an invitation to gather around the hearth which activates the entire living space beyond.

To keep these spaces from becoming too formal or even mundane, the New Native house presses across the plan and cuts open the rooms by using lowered walls, large windows and undulating ceiling heights.

Crib Barn

Crib barns are work buildings. While this label seems obvious, it is important to the New Native house because its other sources (dogtrot, saddle bag, etc.) are residential structures. In this company the *crib barn* is a folk building that is unique. The transverse crib is a building for storing corn and other feed and its appeal is bold and striking.

Typically a center axis is established along which are arranged the "cribs." When the cribs are made of hand-hewn logs the solidity of their volume is dramatic when compared with the "emptiness" of the adjacent aisle ways.

If modern architecture can be said to have used the buildings of industry as its main inspiration, then the *crib barn* is a "modern" reference. It is, after all, a building of pure utility and in that single purpose it informs the New Native house with its reminder of bare geometry. The square and the triangle have never been clearer as forms found in the cribs and sheds of its construction.

> **To keep these spaces from becoming too formal or even mundane, the New Native house presses across the plan and cuts open the rooms by using lowered walls, large windows and undulating ceiling heights.**

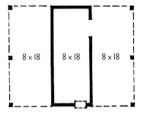

8 x 18   8 x 18   8 x 18

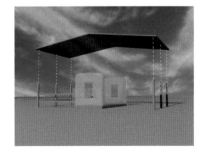

(Top Left) Photo of traditional Crib Barn

(Above Left) Computer rendering of Crib Barn

(Top Right) Plan of Crib Barn

(Above Right) Computer rendering revealing the single roof overhang

No matter how
abstract the calculus
of our advanced world
becomes there is
always place, and the
collective tapestry of
any place results in
a context.

The Rice house, for example, finds its configuration from the *crib barn* memory. The plan is anchored around and along a central concrete element we refer to as the "spine." Its location and its long narrow shape are much like the aisle ways that are found running down the middle of a *crib barn* serving as the backbone for the plan. The rooms attached along the front elevation at the Rice house are at least hinting at the individual "cribs" that would be found in a row down the side of a barn. The shed roof of a barn can also be found in part at both the Irwin and Lisa-Noel Residences as "minor quotes" from the old crib roofs.

The *crib barn* is in many ways the easiest connection to the "modern" vision. A boldly formed shed roof is often used and there is surely no ornament. It is from here that the New Native house can utilize the human capability to reduce and abstract, thus integrating the clarity of the rational with the mystery of the old saddlebag and the dogtrot. Then abstract forms of pure functionality can blend with the more mysterious pieces of the old folk houses.

LOCAL CONTEXT (Soul)

There is always a site for every architectural project, and it is always *somewhere*; not *nowhere*. Thus every house is from somewhere, and that somewhere has a landscape, and that landscape has shape, texture, aroma, contour, flora, fauna, sky, and ground. Inevitably it also possesses the elements of human culture such as buildings, bridges, culverts, fences, walls, poles, tanks, silos, and towers.

In this way, no matter how abstract the calculus of our advanced world becomes there is always *place,* and the collective tapestry of any place results in a *context.* The New Native house is always the quotient of the immediate ingredients of its location translated and distilled through the mechanism of my impressions.

The subject of local context will always worry the educated—progressive mind. After all, it is being *provincial* that is feared the most. The smallness of the mind, local bigotry or the narrow traditions of vernacular life are all daunting to the "traveled" personality who strives for intellectual control and a fashionable sense of tolerance in their view of life. In all of this there is, at least, one very striking paradox; arguably *everything starts in the provinces.*

Whether it be *haute couture* denim that more than a century ago was the miner's tent fabric or the sophisticated orchestrations of Duke Ellington's music that had its origin in the work song of the delta cotton fields, the beginnings of these advanced expressions is more often that not; *local*.

The New Native house finds its soul at the "sweet spot" on the land in a very specific place that must always be located at the start of each project. This specificity of position is true at every site and demands a responsive answer; it asks for a real "location." Ultimately, as I process the context of each dwelling, it is a dialogue that I am seeking; between the new house and its older neighbors.

INTERNATIONAL MODERN ARCHITECTURE (Intellect)

One promise of the modern dream, to end the confinement and darkness of the 19th c. house, is always present in the New Native. Plan and section can be shaped freely, metaphor and symbols can enter, and the devices of the 20th c. can be woven into the composition. Plate glass, layering of spaces, daylight-as-notation, cantilevers, floated objects and painterly surfaces are all available to each scheme as I move it through its stages of incubation.

The spirit of modern architecture for me remains the liberation of the dark, gray building of times past into the free play of the lonely painter or the hopeful musician or the eternal child. The New Native house embraces this potential without becoming a laboratory or a proving ground. The human life of the occupant can be enhanced by these possibilities and then the house can flower. I have found no need to make spaces that are only ideological; but the modern flow of sunlit rooms from inside the heart of house out into the landscape is irresistible even to the most conservative client.

The international stance is available to all of us wherever we turn. (Automobiles, internet, fashion, electronics, cinema, etc.) The New Native house attempts a deep embodiment of these challenges. The global impulse appears in these buildings as a metropolitan spirit that I hope is whispering; "the clean edge" or "the shadows in glass" or "the intrigue of an urban evening."

It is these tantalizing images that the modernist vision has given us. This bold new reality becomes the other partner, along with the vernacular, that joins energy to generate the New Native dwelling.

> The spirit of modern architecture for me remains the liberation of the dark, gray building of times past into the free play of the lonely painter or the hopeful musician or the eternal child. The New Native house embraces this potential without becoming a laboratory or a proving ground.

To the extent that the modernist house was (and is) analytical, the New Native house is also holistic and intuitive. Spaces can be intentionally familiar, and while there is an effort to make the house a compelling object there is an equal desire to build a series of experiences that are serene, intimate and some might say, nurturing.

NATURAL MATERIALS (Body)

Although headed in this direction all along, it is particularly since World War II that the miracle of technology as used by the building products industry has steadily degraded the quality and beauty of the materials used in residential construction. For more than fifty years earnest salesman with polished shoes and three-ring binders have pressed their way into the supply houses, architect's offices and contractors construction trailers extolling the benefits of the newest materials.

Ah, the genius of the free market; cheaper materials, lighter materials and materials that never deteriorate. And the builders, measuring success mostly by the size of their profits, have been eager to facilitate the constant "de-contenting" (taking material out) of the houses they build in exchange for the body and soul of the house. Thus there appears pressed cellulose doors replace solid wood ones, new assemblies are made thinner and thinner, and cheap broadloom carpet is used instead of hardwood floors with the cumulative effect becoming a grim and flimsy picture.

One other benefit of the free market is our collective ability to say no. To these degenerations the New Native house quietly says no. As I have evolved in my selection of materials, the clear truth has spoken time and time again; natural materials (stone, hardwoods, cedar, clay brick, copper, etc.) are more beautiful, have a richer presence and in the larger calculation of an entire project (and an entire life) are easily afforded. The juxtaposition of two, well-chosen, materials can often provide the inspiration for a house well-made and a life well-lived.

BALANCING OPPOSITE FORCES (Spirit)

"The manifest world is a world of opposites-of pleasure versus pain, up versus down, good versus evil, subject versus object, light versus shadow.... But there is a way to be free of the opposites.... Spirit is the great Player that gives rise to all those opposites equally.... Liberation [can occur] when we cease the impossible, painful dream of spending our entire lives trying to find an up without a down, an inside without an outside, a good without an evil, a pleasure without its inevitable pain." —Ken Wilber

It is the New Native house that, for me, becomes the platform on which the richness of opposite elements can find unity; at least momentarily. The legendary houses of my teachers (Villa Mairea, Villa Savoye, Farnsworth, Falling Water, etc.) were masterstrokes from the extreme edge of the spectrum. Analytical, forceful and largely masculine they all possess a long list of stimulating breakthroughs and bold innovations. Alternatively, the New Native in the Modern house has had to represent a different realm; the rest of the continuum.

What does this mean? This means that to the extent that the modernist house was (and is) analytical, the New Native house is also holistic and intuitive. Spaces can be intentionally familiar, and while there is an effort to make the house a compelling object there is an equal desire to build a series of experiences that are serene, intimate and some might say, nurturing.

The balancing of opposite forces in the New Native house takes the form of physical interweaving. Rather than the "use of opposites" ("figure and ground" or "solid and void") there is the desire for a democracy of elements and conditions. A main living room can be fashioned to feel both open to the landscape and intimate and secure, simultaneously. By shaping space and opening walls in just the right way the experience of living in the house can strike a deeper balance between radical confrontations (the cantilevered-glass room) and mundane flatness (the carpet and drywall den).

As the composition evolves, the interdependent materials and spaces can conspire to support an overall sense of Spirit and tranquility; which in the truest sense has no opposite. For those living there, this takes the house from mere shelter or "proud-possession" to an authentic inspiration and thus; balance.

MINDFUL BUDGETS (Society)

The New Native house has the economics necessary allowing affordability to ordinary people. The majority of these houses were completed for under $700,000 and, in fact, two of them for less than $300,000. Because of the use of simple detailing and straightforward geometries the construction of a New Native house has been accomplished on most occasions by contractors who were of "standard" experience with materials that are available at many suppliers.

At right is a sample budget showing the proportionality of expenditures across the various items that comprise the builder's responsibilities.

The architectural fee is shown on the last three lines of the budget and totals $12.00 per square foot. I have found that the calculation of the architectural fee is perceived by the owner as fairer if its value is tied to the total square footage

Typical Budget

1. Excavation	1.00 / S.F.
2. Crushed Stone	1.50 / S.F.
3. Footings and Foundations	3.25 / S.F.
4. Concrete Floors	2.25 / S.F.
5. Termite Control	.25 / S.F.
6. Lumber Package	20.25 / S.F.
7. Doors and Windows	9.00 / S.F.
8. Framing Labor	14.00 / S.F.
9. Plumbing	2.25 / S.F.
10. Electrical	2.00 / S.F.
11. Heating and Cooling	2.75 / S.F.
12. Septic System	1.60 / S.F.
13. Site Utilities	.75 / S.F.
14. Insulation	1.25 / S.F.
15. Brick Material	4.75 / S.F.
16. Brick Labor	3.40 / S.F.
17. Special Fireplace	2.90 / S.F.
18. Exterior Trim	5.20 / S.F.
19. Metal Roof	1.90 / S.F.
20. Drywall	4.80 / S.F.
21. Interior Trim	4.75 / S.F.
22. Ceramic Tile	1.75 / S.F.
23. Hardwood Flooring	1.50 / S.F.
24. Fees & Dumpster	.25 / S.F.
25. Cabinetry (kitchen, etc.)	5.00 / S.F.
26. Plumbing fixtures	3.00 / S.F.
27. Light Fixtures	1.60 / S.F.
28. Door Hardware	.75 / S.F.
29. Painting	4.00 / S.F.
30. Carpet	2.25 / S.F.
31. Misc. Details	1.75 / S.F.
32. Architectural Design	5.00 / S.F.
33. Contract Documents (drawings and specifications)	5.00 / S.F.
34. Construction Phase Services	2.00 / S.F.
TOTAL BUDGET PER SQUARE FOOT	$123.00

Note: In order to accurately calculate a total dollar amount all floor areas must be included (i.e. garages, basements, porches) Note that construction costs vary by location and circumstance. For example: New York and California will be higher.

Bill Evans and Miles Davis, 1958. Davis made *integral music*. Evans brought Europe, Davis brought Africa and the recording known as Kind of Blue was *world* music.

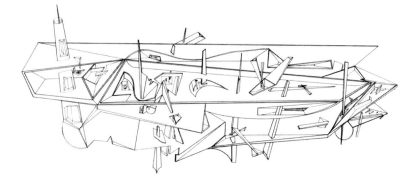

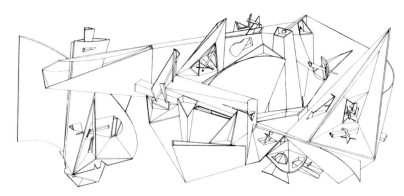

(Top) House for a Cartographer, Project, 1982, Scott L. Guyon, Architect

(Bottom) Community Building for a Small City, Project, 1983, Scott L. Guyon, Architect

rather than the traditional percentage of construction value. The square footage method alleviates the concern that the architect is "choosing" expensive materials in order to inflate his fee and it properly emphasizes the architect's work as reflecting size and complexity rather than luxury and expense.

There is no more crucial element to the viability of these houses than the ability to reassure and confirm a workable budget. It is a virtual certainty that the owner's acceptance of the value of the architectural services will be dependent upon cost-containment and predictable budgets. The poetics of the New Native house have always had to pass on to the owner as a "windfall" benefit in what is otherwise a very practical process.

INTEGRAL ARCHITECTURE Radical Balance not Radical Form

In the continuous search to spell out and shape the "New Native," sources and inspirations entered my mind as a series of small impressions (empty fields, mediocre suburbs, majestic churches, etc.). These impressions seem disparate and unrelated. Why would this condition of variety and fragmentation concern me so strongly? One word ... imbalance.

The inspiration to discover an *integral architecture* was (and is) the simple desire to create balance. Why? To dissuade the un-integrated from my world; to move beyond the contemporary fascination with anxiety and chaos. A truly silent room can do this. This collection of houses is an offering to that cause.

My first encounter with the experience of essence and balance did not happen in Architecture. It came to me in jazz music as played by Miles Davis and Bill Evans. Davis and Evans knew how to balance; and they knew how to synthesize. Davis understood our collective desire for beauty and soul, and he understood essence as a process of leaving behind the extra and superfluous. Evans brought a tenderness of feeling and a highly sophisticated intelligence to what and how he played. In their music, one can find the true meaning of the word *integral*. Evans brought the European; Davis the African, and together they made a music that was global. In this way, the spaces and the silences of their integral music become schematic for my gestures and sketches as I start these New Native houses. Nothing extra and nothing left out is the verse I give to all my clients.

To arrive at an essential stillness one has to know something about frenzy. Looking back twenty years, I remember two projects that I developed in 1982 and 1983. The House for a Cartographer and A Community Building for a Small City (see illustration previous page bottom left) represent hard-riding and wide-ranging expressions of the "shaped vessel" or the "plasticity-of-the-heart." In these projects I dove into hyper-plasticity to see if it would sustain me. It did; but not quite. These experiments in space and form are my effort to feed an impulse that desires a meaningful object.

The necessity of this creative impulse did not go away with the passage of time. The desire or the lust for the "original" is within all of us. The original form as a passion can eventually soften or naturally appear as something redis-covered from the past. A deeper desire can emerge; a way of making form that is not less expressive, but one that is more inclusive.

THE DEEPLY BALANCED In the New Native House

Integral architecture is, of course, an aspiration. And as a living vision it cannot be reduced to a formula of methods or a set of materials. As I have sought a clearer understanding of the world around me it has followed that the cycles of balance in the natural world are unavoidable. Temperatures, rainfall amounts, animal populations, seasonal daylight and countless other conditions in our world are continuously and constantly balancing.

In the constructed world of the New Native house (or any building) there can be an emulation of these natural cycles. In the incorporation of these cycles I have arrived at what can be called the interwoven space. This way of

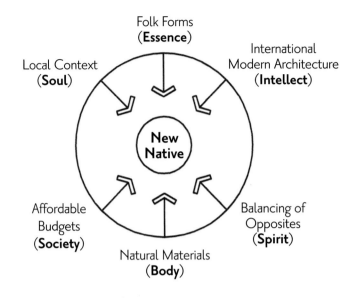

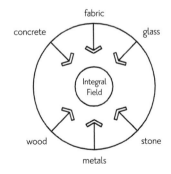

Integration of Materials

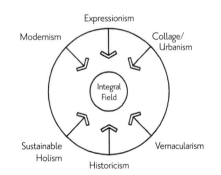

Integration of Architectural Movements

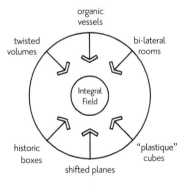

Integration of Space-Form Types

True Architecture remains an idea, not a material style. Those who reach into their deepest passion, toward some divinity beyond their personalities, those individual architects will occasionally unleash the magnificent. Their space will synchronize with the universe's unfathomable mystery and it will stop our daily world: forcing us out own small lives and revealing a vastness far beyond our logic or our reason.
—Scott Guyon

The Houses

Scott L. Guyon, Architect
Paul Swisher, Project Architect

Office Support Team 1990–2003

Mike Barry	Ken Koett	Will Nash
Rafael E. Bedolla	Rick Jones	Robert Tate Overton
Martha Hutchison Bono	Jeremiah Joseph	Nich Passafiume
Chrisitan Brantner	Chris Keesling	Jon Rollins
Marina Dillion	Brian Lindroth	Sarah Ryan
Bob Gillig	Gene McDonald	David Silvernell
Sydney Goetz	Jason Merrick	Mike Sparkman
Carey Hirt	Frieda Meyer	Jerome Tobias
Dale Hockenberry	Michael Meyer	Kari White
Joshua R. Ives	Leah Moore	
Daimin Japar	Ashley Musgrave	

designing and forming starts as nothing more than an "intention to reconcile." The reconciliation is between the forces and conditions found within each project.

In the making of space there is always the choice of how it should be shaped. Perhaps the space could be a simple box or, alternatively, it could be animated and energized by a gesture that is sweeping and dramatic. In the New Native the choice has been made. And in that decision is my belief that a *space is most integrated when it is at rest*. These spaces at rest can then become the 'field' on which the complexity of the world will play. As an example consider the phenomenon of daylight. The sun and its movements can freely mark a constantly changing line on the wall surfaces of any room. Thus, by consciously positioning a wall surface as a receptor for the sunlight the constructed "wall" declares its relationship with the sun.

This, by itself, is not new in architecture. What can be a new discovery are the endless combinations of these simple relationships. When joined together they express a sense of quiet beauty and lively silence that can be sacred. Glass, stone and wood, to name a few key materials, can begin to resonate with this balance if they are used with their essential qualities in mind. In a New Native house this means simpler geometries and fewer and fewer materials until the unnecessary is moved out of sight and then; the realm beyond these materials might occasionally reveal itself. The deep balance ultimately resides in the invisible feeling one receives by residing in a beautiful room. That feeling is found beyond the physical materials, somewhere in the realm of spirit. This notion of balance and integration does not require homogeneity. It is simply the intention toward balance that makes the difference. Any person or any architect will always possess his or her own voice and its exact expression will be physically unique. But in the desire to balance and to deeply integrate our environment a thoughtful building can support an awakening toward a wider and truly liberated life.

New Native Houses

Size: 2800 sq.ft.

Major Materials
    Metal Barn Roof
    Concrete Brick
    Oak Floor

Old Source: Dogtrot House
New Source: Datum roof with under volume

Taylor Residence
Georgetown, Kentucky
1992

I began this project by making a composite reinterpretation of the cottage dwellings that can be seen in the horse farm landscape of Kentucky. Beyond the local vernacular, there are farm buildings to be found in other rolling landscapes (Tuscany for example) that inspired my search.

The house fits the American dream programmatically (i.e. 3 bedrooms, 2 ½ bathrooms & garage) but it was also constructed of entirely standard items from local suppliers at $93 a square foot. This fulfills my long-standing desire to offer to an average person a house that contains carefully shaped spaces and unashamedly poetic associations at the same cost as a standard "tract" house. For me, this affordability does not lower the stakes of the project architecturally it actually enriches and enhances them.

The house is conceived as a free-playing series of spaces positioned beneath a folded and carved master roof. This roof extends beyond the body of the building and sits on raw wood columns creating porches front and back. Daylight is invited in through cut-in flaps that appear as dormers.

(Above) View of front elevation across meadow

(Opposite) West entry elevation; reminiscent of the dogtrot

Site plan

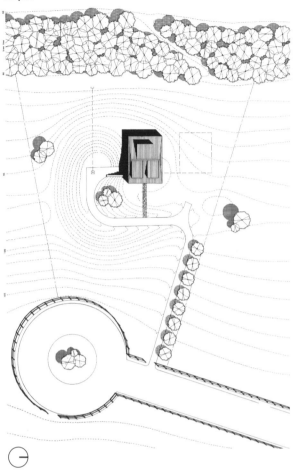

East entry elevtation with screened-in porch

East Elevation

West Elevation

South elevation with porches front and back

3-Dimensional Renderings

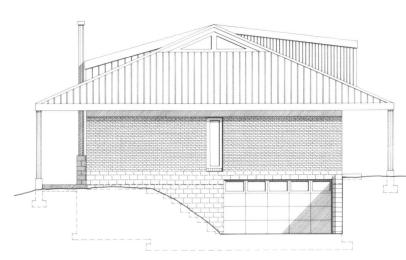

South Elevation

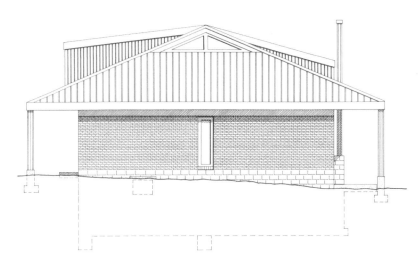

North Elevation

Roof Plan

Second Floor Plan

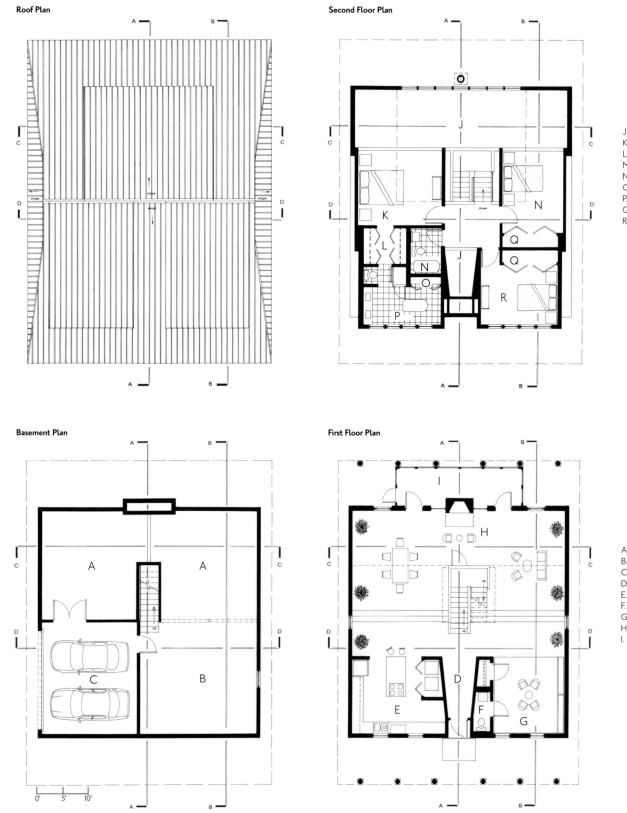

J. Open to Below
K. Master Bedroom
L. Dressing
M. Linen
N. Guest Bedroom
O. Linen
P. Master Bath
Q. Closet
R. Guest Bedroom

Basement Plan

First Floor Plan

A. Storage
B. Workshop
C. Garage
D. Entry
E. Kitchen
F. Half Bath
G. Den/Study
H. Great Room
I. Screened Porch

0'   5'   10'

(Above) View of entry elevation and surrounding site across meadow

Building section through fireplace and centrat stair

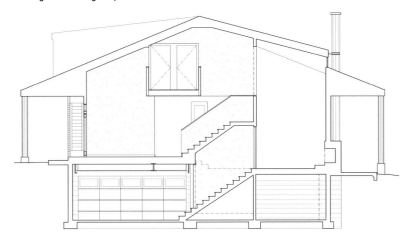

Building section through great room looking towad kitchen

Building section through great room, den, and guest room

Building section through bedrooms looking toward great room

(Above) View toward dining area along rear wall

(Right) View of dining area with living space beyond

(Opposite) Kitchen and Dining

(Left) View of stair from front door

(Bottom Left) View of stair from den

(Bottom Right) Stair Landing

Size: 2200 sq.ft.

Major Materials
    Metal Barn Roof
    Western Red Cedar
    Oak Floor

Source: Two Front Door Tenant House
New Source: Additive volume with cuts

Coughlin Residence
Versailles, Kentucky
1994

The Coughlin house aspires to make clear 'place' in the rolling landscape. The scheme makes one move to the right in order to position the garage element. This allows the hedgerow to the north and the virtual edge of the view to the east to provide the closure required to define the raised courtyard that separates the house from the territory beyond.

The house is divided into three zones on the first level that completely satisfy the needs of a single owner. There is one section for the master suite, one for the cooking and dining, and one for living and relaxing.

Kentucky is not the theatrical Northeast nor is it the melodramatic West Coast; Kentucky is the center. This is the simple reality of the American sky separated downward by the solid ground where, as Wright said, common sense can become a work of Art.

(Above) View of front elevation across lake

(Opposite) Rear elevation and "saddlebag" porch

Site Plan

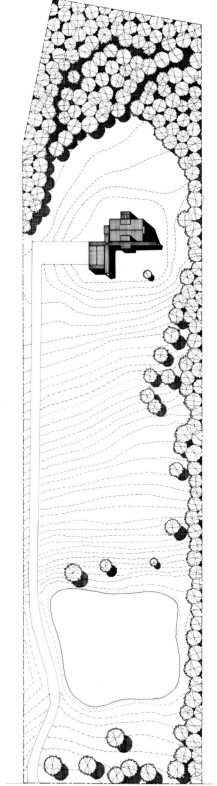

Second Floor Plan

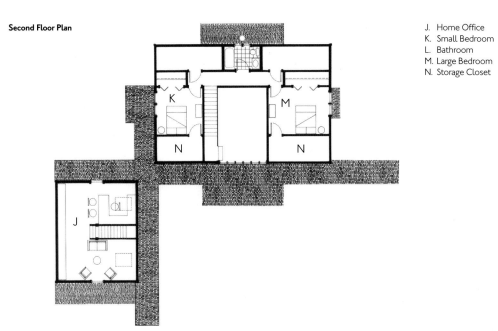

J. Home Office
K. Small Bedroom
L. Bathroom
M. Large Bedroom
N. Storage Closet

First Floor Plan

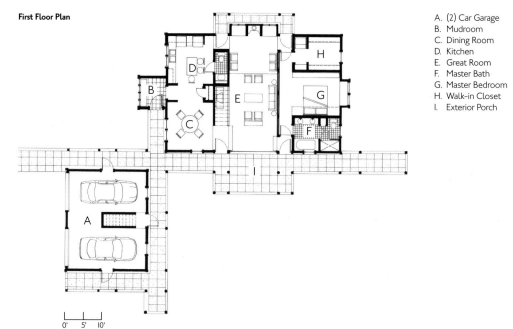

A. (2) Car Garage
B. Mudroom
C. Dining Room
D. Kitchen
E. Great Room
F. Master Bath
G. Master Bedroom
H. Walk-in Closet
I. Exterior Porch

0'   5'   10'

Building section through great room and fireplace

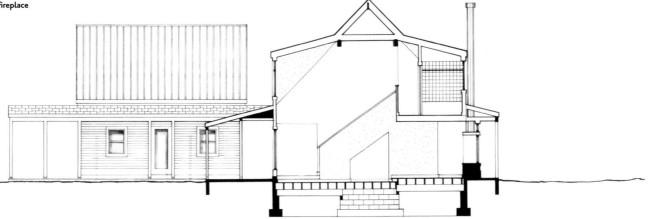

Building section through garage and home office

Sketch of house across lake

3-Dimensional Renderings

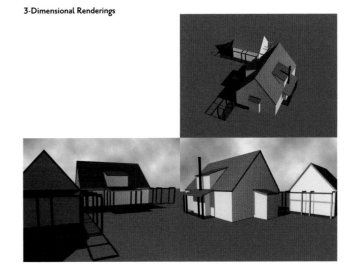

(Above) View of Northeast courtyard

(Left) View of Southwest courtyard

(Opposite Left) View of main house porch/colonnade

(Opposite Right) View of garage porch/colonnade

(Above) View from balcony toward front porch

(Right) View of great room toward fireplace

(Left) View of kitchen

(Right) View of glass viewing window at entry

(Left) View of fireplace in great room

(Right) View of cut-out under stair in great room

(Following Page) View through main glass window

Size: 1600 sq.ft.

Major Materials
  Metal Barn Roof
  Western Red Cedar
  Poplar

Old Source: Double Pen House
New Source: Clustered Volumes

Burgess-Smith Residence
Sadieville, Kentucky
1995

As part of the process of design for this cabin-in-the-forest, I was drawn again to the folk houses of the Old South. The dogtrot, the saddlebag, the shotgun and the double pen were plan forms that rolled around in my memory and provided a poetic source for the strategy used to fashion the early sketches for this project.

The site is on the crest of a Kentucky knob located above Eagle Creek in the Eden hills of Scott County. The plan consists of two identical gabled volumes each twenty by thirty feet. The five-foot zone that separates the two pieces is thought of as "going clear through" and probably recalls the dogtrot space seen in many early southern houses.

The volume to the south contains all the community functions (living, cooking, dining) and the volume to the north contains the more private activities (four sleeping rooms and two baths). All told the plan comprises about 1500 square feet that is placed along the ridge and faces down the slope toward an Indian mound and the creek below.

This is a house of simple spaces set freely in the sunlight and dressed in cedar wood with a barn roof. To my surprise, it looks both ways; toward remembrances of some things past while still insisting on this day and time including the freedom of space given to us by the modern house.

(Above) View of approach with slot at entry

(Opposite) View of west elevation

Site Plan

Perspective sketch of front, north elevation

South Elevation

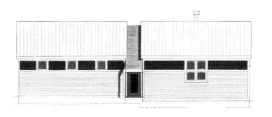

East Elevation

3-Dimensional Renderings

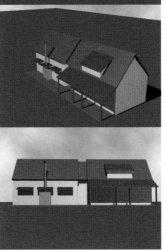

North Elevation

West Elevation

Second Floor Plan

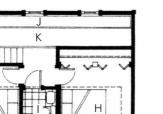

H. Bedroom
I. Bath
J. Shelf
K. Open to Below

First Floor Plan

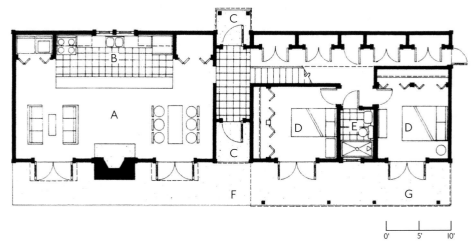

A. Livng Room/Dining Room
B. Kitchen
C. Entry
D. Bedroom
E. Bath
F. Open Porch
G. Cover Porch

0'   5'   10'

(Above) View toward main facade with "dogtrot" slot
at center

(Opposite Top) View of entry door

(Opposite Bottom) View along south side toward
entry door

(Left) View of the top of stairs toward living room

(Right) View of living room toward stair

View of fireplace

View of north elevation at night

Size: 2850 sq.ft.

Major Materials
Metal Barn Roof
Western Red Cedar
Redwood

Old Source: Dogtrot House
New Source: Hyphenated Transparency

Lisa-Noel Residence
Shelby Lane, Fayette County, Kentucky
1997

The Lisa-Noel House presented itself as a building on a ridge with the surrounding site to remain as a naturalized bramble. The dogtrot plan played against my desire to push forward with a contemporary building. The owners, two botanists, vowed never to mow or manicure the hillside and asked to leave all the exterior wood unstained so that it would just gray and weather into a very rustic patina.

The plan is arranged on two levels that add up to about 2,800 square feet with a master bedroom area at the end of the first level and the public living spaces placed around the large chimney that also serves as the "anchor" for the stairway. The saddle-bag type can be seen influencing the core of the house while the transparent slots that pass through at the garage and the front door are traced to the dogtrot. This little house is long and slender and is imagined to be sailing across the wave of the pasture that is set out beyond a large horse farm to the north and a few barns and silos going south.

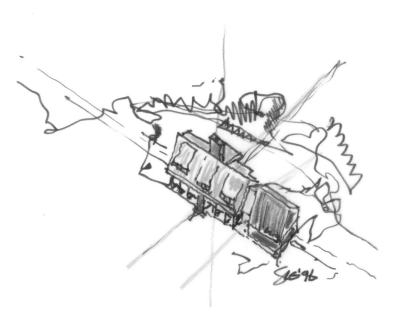

(Above) View of house across horse farm

(Opposite) View of northwest corner in meadow

Site Plan

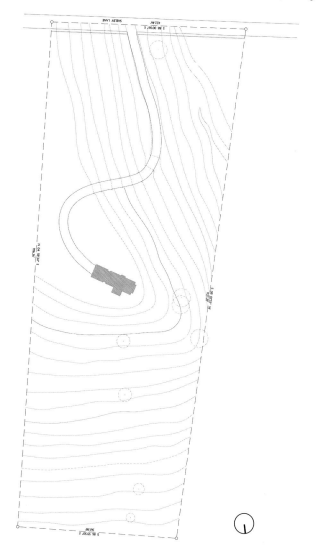

(Right) View of southwest corner

(Below Right) Photo of model

West Elevation

East Elevation

North Elevation

South Elevation

3-Dimensional Renderings

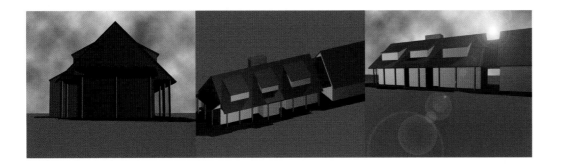

Building section through fireplace, living room, entry

Building section through length of house

Building section through bedrooms

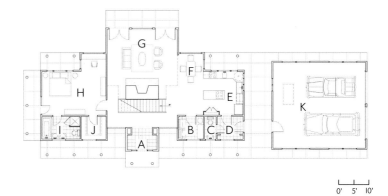

Second Floor Plan

First Floor Plan

0' 5' 10'

L. Hall Bath
M. Den
N. Bedroom
O. Attic Storage

A. Front Entry
B. Laundry
C. Half Bath
D. Mudroom
E. Kitchen
F. Dining Area
G. Living Room
H. Master Bedroom
I. Master Bath
J. Walk-in Closet
K. Garage

View of north elevation

(Opposite) View of fireplace from living room

(Above) View of living room and porch beyond

(Above Left) View of living room toward fireplace

(Above Right) View of second floor corridor toward den

View of bookshelves in second floor corridor

View of north elevation at night

Size: 3400 sq.ft.

Major Materials
  Metal Barn Roof
  Red Brick & Mortar
  Redwood Columns
  Oak Floors

Old Source: Two Front Door Tenant House
New Source: Phenomenal Transparency

Shepherd Residence
Paris, Kentucky
1998

The Shepherd presented the notion of a single folded roof that, if devised skillfully enough, would elegantly hover above the simple program of this plan. The main spaces are located along the entry axis with the master bedroom to the South and the garage to the North.

The owners had asked for a kind of mezzanine above the main living space on which they could have a game room. It suddenly occurred to me that this could be seen as an inversion (in section) of the American-basement that usually finds this use by default.

As with other houses in this series, I have used a language of form and material intended to recognize several dreams at once. In the main living areas you find the free play of space and transparency associated with modernism while on the front and rear elevations there is the memory of the porches found in old tenant houses. The metal barn-roof, limestone chimney, and redwood porch columns are all intended to urge the owners to enjoy the intensified richness of primary and down-to-earth materials set against the more aloof feelings of precision metals, angular spaces and large expanses of plate glass.

(Above) Rear elevation as seen from across the meadow

(Opposite) View of south elevation

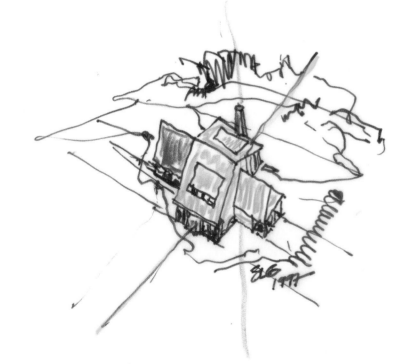

Site Plan

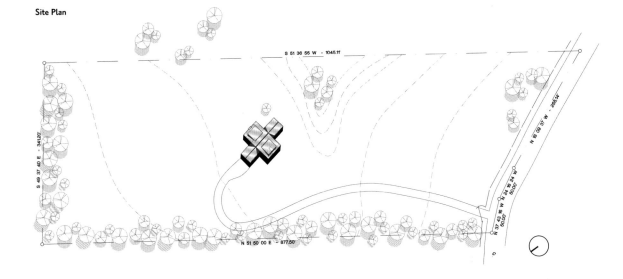

3-Dimensional Renderings

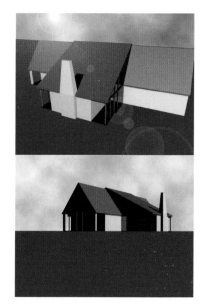

Building section through garage and master bedroom

Building section through entry, great room, fireplace

West Elevation

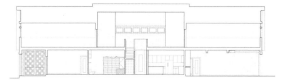

South Elevation

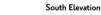

East Elevation

(Top) View of chimney and great room window

(Above) View of northwest corner

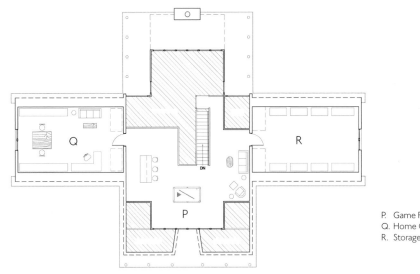

P. Game Room
Q. Home Office
R. Storage

First Floor Plan

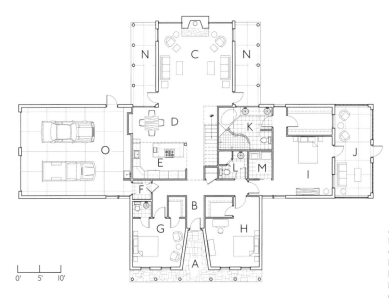

0' 5' 10'

A. Front Porch
B. Entry Foyer
C. Great Room
D. Dining Room
E. Kitchen
F. Mudroom
G. Guest Room Suite
H. Bedroom
I. Master Bedroom
J. Screened Porch
K. Master Bath
L. Hall Bath
M. Laundry Room
N. Side Porches
O. Garage

(Top) View of west elevation

(Above) View of north elevation

View of west elevation

View of living room area and porch beyond from balcony

View of living area toward kitchen

View of living area toward fireplace and porch beyond

View of master bath

Size: 3150 sq.ft.

Major Materials
  Metal Barn Roof
  Western Red Cedar
  Redwood Columns
  Red Brick & Mortar
  Oak Floors
  Maple Cabinetry

Old Source: Saddlebag House
New Source: Neo-Plastic Extension Outward

Jackson-Vance Residence
Turkey Foot, Kentucky
2000

The sharply rolling landscape of northern Kentucky provides the backdrop for this house and its inhabitants. My early sketches of this project revolved around the "anchoring" brick chimney and the creation of a space (garden) between the building and the rugged farmland beyond.

The plan-form arose from the folk house known as the "saddlebag" in which the central chimney provides the main support for the surrounding spaces. Since the house was designed for two retired friends the program requires two of everything. Thus; two gardens, two garage stalls, two offices, two master suites and two belvederes at the front porch that create a balance and equality for both owners.

The materials are from the "New Native" palette with metal barn roofing, western red cedar siding (linseed oil finish), redwood columns and a red brick chimney.

I have sought to make a small and quiet universe in and around this house and in so doing move again toward the essence of naturalness that allows the building and gardens to rest easily on the top of this wooded ridge.

(Above) View of east elevation and landscape

(Opposite) View of east elevation

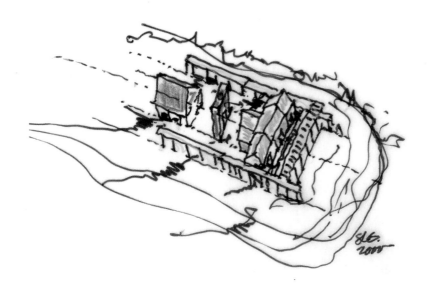

North Elevation

3-Dimensional Renderings

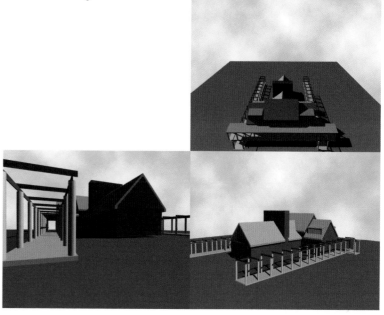

South Elevation

Section

West Elevation

Section

Site Plan

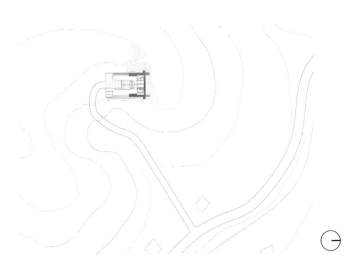

First Floor Plan

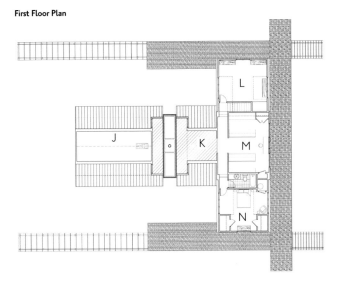

J. Loft Storage
K. Great Room Below
L. Storage
M. Library
N. Guest Room

(Below) Photo of model

(Bottom) View of entrance

Second Floor Plan

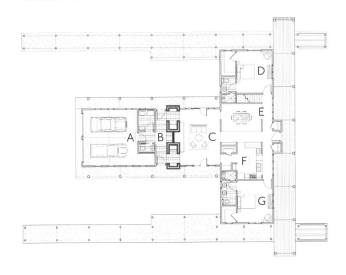

A. Garage
B. Mudroom
C. Great Room
D. Master Bedroom
E. Dining Area
F. Kitchen
G. Master Bedroom
H. Entry
I. Front Porch

0' 5' 10'

(Opposite) View of east elevation across field

(Top) View of front porch on east elevation

(Above) View of meadow across front elevation with belvedere

View of fireplace from balcony

View of great room from balcony

(Above) View of great room toward fireplace

(Next page) View of house and landscape

Size: 4082 sq.ft.

Major Materials
    Metal Barn Roof
    Western Red Cedar
    Cedar Columns
    Limestone Dry Stack Foundation
    Oak Floors
    Maple Cabinetry

Old Source: Saddlebag House with Sheds
New Source: Volumes attached to linear spine

Polmanteer Residence
Madison County, Kentucky
2002

The horse country of Madison County, Kentucky provides the site for this house and its numerous out-buildings. The views to the south are inspiring and frame the 'pinnacles' thirty miles away in Berea, Kentucky.

The scheme uses the saddlebag folk house again as a reference for the plan of the main building. The colonnade that connects the garage, guesthouse, and dining pavilion is a simple 'spine' along which small volumes attach themselves. This aggregation of small buildings invites the making of garden spaces between one and the other. This spatial layout offers the reassuring experience of the cloister with views across the courtyards and into other parts of the house beyond.

The materials are from the 'New Native' vocabulary and include metal barn roofing, cedar shake roofing, western red cedar siding (bleached finish) and cedar columns.

The little village of buildings arranges itself on a line projected west from a large oak tree. This tree terminates the colonnade and positions the buildings along the slope of the pasture so that time will allow them to become as 'original' as the landscape itself.

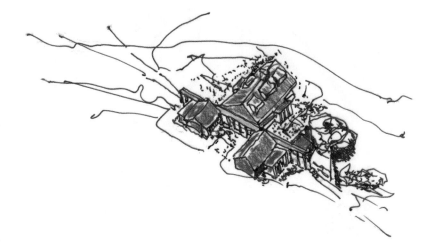

(Above) View of east elevation

(Opposite) View of west elevation

Building section through great room and dining pavilion

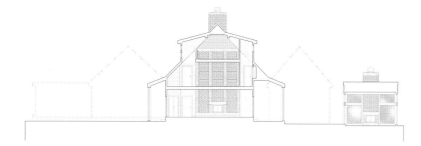

3-Dimensional Renderings

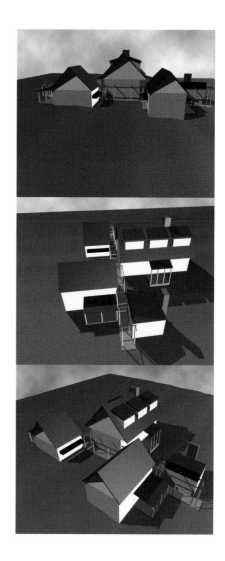

Building section through garage and shop

North Elevation

South Elevation

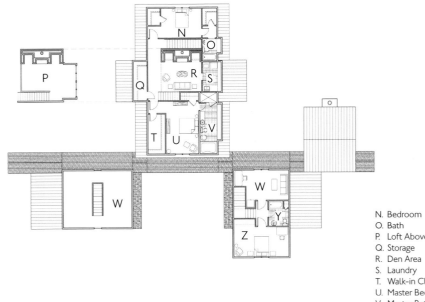

Second Floor Plan

N. Bedroom
O. Bath
P. Loft Above Den
Q. Storage
R. Den Area
S. Laundry
T. Walk-in Closet
U. Master Bedroom
V. Master Bath
W. Attic Storage
X. Home Office
Y. Guest Bath
Z. Guest Bedroom

First Floor Plan

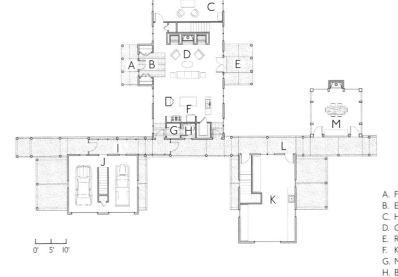

0' 5' 10'

A. Front Porch
B. Entry
C. Home Office
D. Great Room
E. Rear Porch
F. Kitchen
G. Mudroom
H. Bath
I. Sealed Connector
J. Garage
K. Shop
L. Connector
M. Dining Pavilion

(Top) Front of main building

(Bottom) Rear of main building

 Site Plan

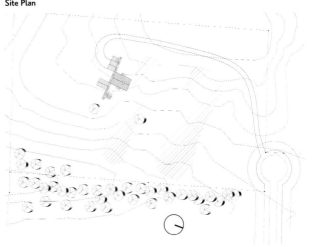

(Opposite clockwise from top left) View of dining pavilion from studio porch, view of dining pavilion across main building's south porch, view of garage from main house

(Above) View of dining pavilion toward studio

(Right) View of southwest elevation

(Previous Page) View of dining pavilion fireplace

(Opposite Top) View of living room from kitchen

(Opposite Bottom) View of kitchen from living room

(Right) View of master bath

(Next Page) View of southwest approach

Size: 2450 sq.ft.

Major Materials
   Metal Barn Roof
   Western Red Cedar
   Cast Concrete
   Maple Cabinetry

Old Source: Tractor Shed
New Source: Master Roof with Articulated Cubic Volumes

Rice Residence
Lexington, Kentucky
2000

The arrangement of a large master roof hovering above a space below seems to be one of the oldest and most elemental to be found in building construction.

The Rice residence contains several storylines but in the language of the "New Native" its genesis can be found in the "work buildings" of the rural South. These buildings include barns, sheds, silos, smokehouses and cribs. Simultaneously, the house also contains a linear 'spine' made of concrete that acts as an armature along which all the spaces of the house are attached. All of the "water elements" (baths, laundry, etc.) of the house are located within this concrete 'spine' and it directs the flow of movement from kitchen to living room to master bedroom along its length from one end of the building to another.

The area for living is a modest 2500 square feet which orients itself toward a wooded wetland and the western sky beyond. Because of this, the intimacy of the room sizes is increased by the openness and daylight that are directed into each space by a series of clustered windows and glass doors that open to the terrace. Its real desire is to reconcile the tough beauty of a barn with the intricacy of modern architecture.

(Top Left) View of northeast elevation

(Opposite) View of southeast elevation

First Floor Plan

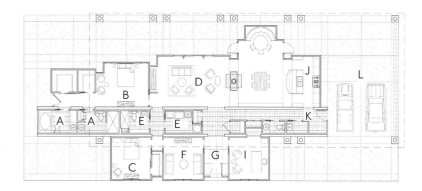

A. Master Bath
B. Master Bedroom
C. Bedroom
D. Living Room
E. Laundry
F. Entertainment Room
G. Entry Area
H. Dining Room
I. Home Office
J. Kitchen
K. Mudroom
L. Carport/Porch

0' 5' 10'

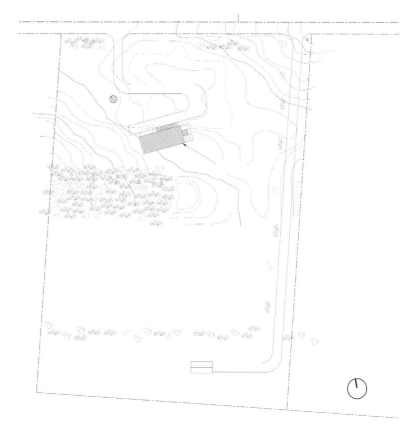

South Elevation

East Elevation

North Elevation

West elevation

Northeast elevation—master bath at end of concrete spine

Building section along concrete spine toward living room

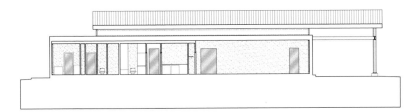

Building section through master bedroom and guest bedroom

Building section through secondary spaces

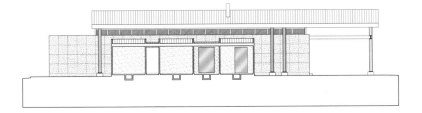

Building section through great room, entry toward fireplace

3-Dimensional Renderings

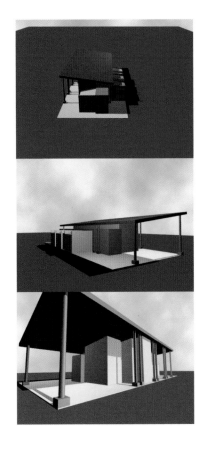

View of concrete "spine" at northeast elevation

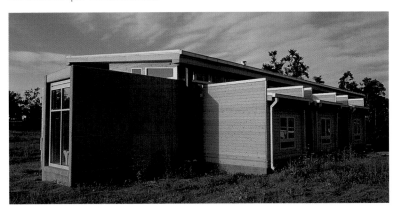

View of northwest elevation

View of southwest elevation

(Left) View down concrete spine toward carport

(Right) View of living room toward kitchen

View of dining room toward living room

View of dining room toward concrete spine

(Above) View of living room from master bedroom

(Right) View of kitchen from dining room

Size: 4500 sq.ft.

Major Materials
  Metal Barn Roof
  Brick
  Oak Floors
  Maple Cabinetry

Old Source: Three Gable Farm House
New Source: Path on axis to terminal object

Meier Residence
Fayette County, Kentucky
1997

In the mid-nineteen eighties I was teaching design studio when I came upon the "mission slogan" for the architecture school at Cooper Union. It tersely defined the study of Architecture as "the search for new forms." Of course at the time, I was fully aware of Louis Kahn's somewhat haunting counter-remark; "what has been will always be."

The Meier House is a transformation of the three-gable I-House. It embodies both the vision of new forms and the poetic power of the old "center hall" plans. This three-gable I-House can be found repeatedly throughout the South mostly built as wood frame.

The house shown here shapes itself around its gables and also offers an emphasis along the entry axis. The canopy assemblage at the front door marks this path of entry and later this line is culminated by the tall fireplace space and further marked by the over-massed chimney.

Both owners are artists so they welcome the use of modern space. In order to animate the main space openings and slots are located at critical points to provide day-lighting necessary for the main living areas. On the second level, their sons' bedrooms are placed up in the gables so that their childhood memories can take advantage of "playing in the attic" as part of everyday life.

(Top Left) View of northeast elevation across meadow

(Opposite) View of northwest elevation with garage entry

South Elevation

Section

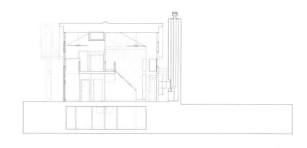

West Elevation

Section

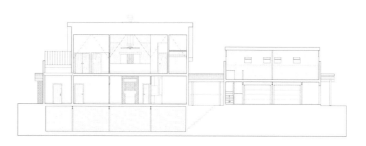

East Elevation

3-Dimensional Renderings

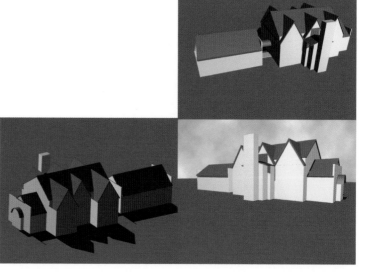

Site Plan

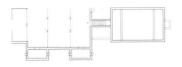

Second Floor Plan

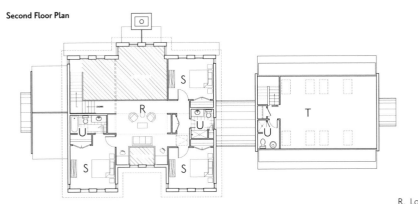

R. Loft Seating Area
S. Bedroom
T. Home Office
U. Bath

First Floor Plan

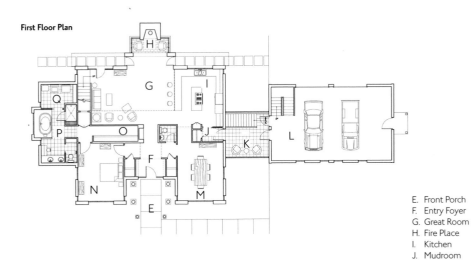

E. Front Porch
F. Entry Foyer
G. Great Room
H. Fire Place
I. Kitchen
J. Mudroom
K. Connector
L. Garage
M. Dining Room
N. Master Bedroom
O. Walk-in Closet
P. Master Bathroom
Q. Laundry Room

View of model

Basement Floor Plan

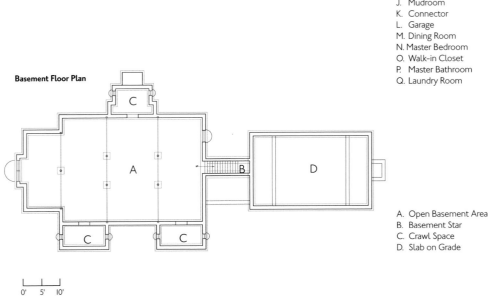

A. Open Basement Area
B. Basement Star
C. Crawl Space
D. Slab on Grade

0'   5'   10'

(Opposite Above) View of west elevation

(Opposite) View of east elevation

(Right) View of entrance canopy

View of living room and fireplace nook from second floor balcony

View of room and fireplace "inglenook" toward stair

View of living room and kitchen bar toward entry

View of living room toward kitchen bar

Size: 7100 sq.ft.

Major Materials
    Metal Barn Roof
    Concrete Brick
    Bamboo Floors
    Maple Cabinetry

Old Source: I-House Woodshed Smokehouse
New Source: Linear Bar with Edged Court

Irwin Residence
Tates Creek, Fayette County, Kentucky
1998

With a ten-acre site, situated in the bluegrass landscape, I was approached by the owners with the challenge of fashioning a meaningful house amidst the drumbeat of the homebuilder "empty-boxes" that hover together in one development after another all over central Kentucky.

This project is located on a beautiful hillside in the contoured landscape of horse farms and country roads adjacent to a major river. The program of 7,100 square feet spoke to me as a caution-flag against bigness. To scale down the long list of spaces it was decided that the main house would "shelf" itself into the natural slope and two "out-buildings" would dispose themselves at the edges of the entry yard making reference to the folk houses of the region where woodsheds and smoke houses are always part of the scene.

The main house generates itself from the old plan-form known as the I-House where a central space acts as an armature for two almost identical wings that arrange themselves on either side. The system of porches that run around the perimeter of the main house provide a kind of "ship's deck" that allows one to step out of the house at any point and take in the constantly changing farmland.

(Above) View of north elevation

(Opposite) View of east elevation

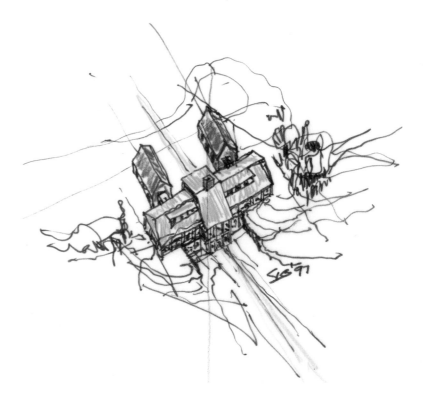

East Elevation

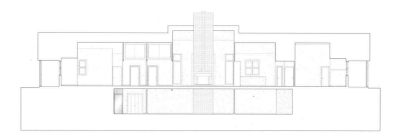

South Elevation

Section

West Elevation

North Elevation

Section

3-Dimensional Renderings

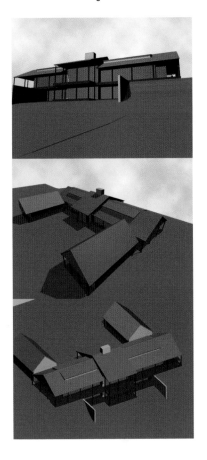

Second Floor Plan

Q. Guest Bedroom
R. Entertainment Area
S. Living Room
T. Sitting Room
U. Workshop

First Floor Plan

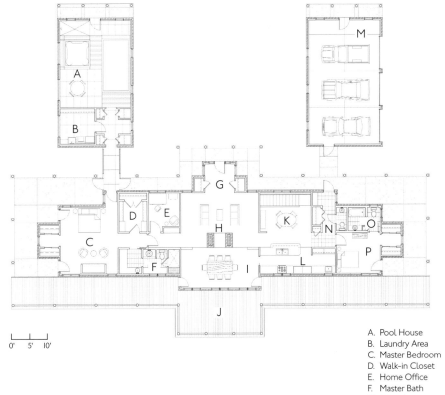

A. Pool House
B. Laundry Area
C. Master Bedroom
D. Walk-in Closet
E. Home Office
F. Master Bath
G. Entry Area
H. Living Room
I. Dining Room
J. Covered Porch
K. Breakfast Area
L. Kitchen
M. Garage
N. Mudroom
O. Bathroom
P. Bedroom

Site Plan

0'   5'   10'

(Left) View of side porch toward pool house link

(Right) View of front porch toward main entry

(Above) View of south elevation

(Previous Page) View of living room toward fireplace

(Previous Page) View of kitchen toward fireplace

View of west elevation and main entrance

West elevation of pool house with main entry beyond

Size: 6900 sq.ft.

Major Materials
  Stucco
  Concrete Brick
  Clay Brick
  Oak Floors

Old Source: Central Passage House
New Source: Aggregation around central locus

Kentucky Residence
Jessamine County, Kentucky
1996

In tackling this rather large program, I was continually struck by the dilemma of how it might be possible to bring real heart and soul to a house that has so many competing aspirations. I have allowed several vocabularies of form to coexist beside and among one another. When conceiving the house, I was reminded of the historical condition of formal "public elevations" and the more relaxed "garden elevations" that can be seen in many Roman villas and in the English cottages (Lutyens, etc.).

The entire main level was placed one foot above the adjacent lake so that major views would always be taken at the level of the water beyond. This house is intended to move and slide as it works its way down the slope. The chimney joins with the stairs to anchor the major turn in the plan while the water views to the south are opened onto the porches.

In the end, the house is formal and then it is informal; it's open and then it is contained; It's low-slung and then it stands up tall, telling us that balance and paradox can be one and the same. Its integration is found in its willingness to entertain many opposites.

(Above) View of west elevation across pond

(Opposite) View of west elevation

Site Plan

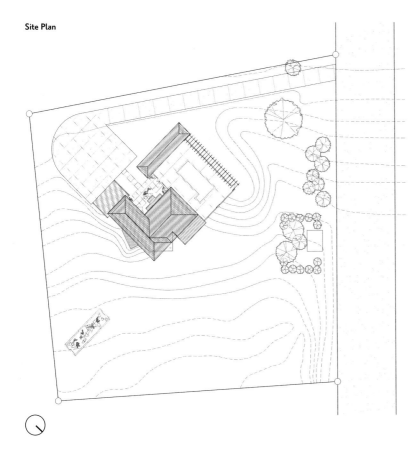

View of north elevation

East Elevation

North Elevation

(Right) View of pool and poolhouse

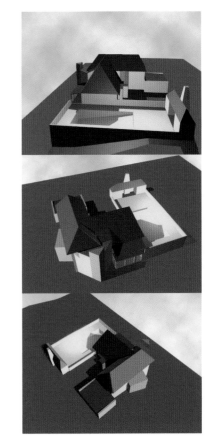

West Elevation

South Elevation

Second Floor Plan

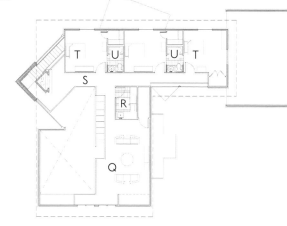

Q. Study above Master Bedroom
R. Laundry Room
S. Balcony Hall
T. Bedroom
U. Bath

First Floor Plan

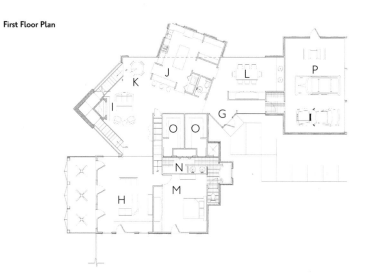

G. Entry
H. Living Room
I. Fireplace
J. Kitchen
K. Breakfast
L. Dining Room
M. Master Bedroom
N. Master Bath
O. Dressing
P. Garage

Basement Floor Plan

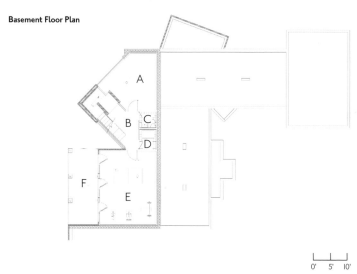

A. Home Office
B. Hall
C. Half Bath
D. Mechanical Room
E. Game Room
F. Lower Porch

0'   5'   10'

(Right) View of west elevation

(Top) View of living room from balcony toward fireplace

(Above) View of living room from stair   (Opposite) View of stair wrapping fireplace

(Right) View of dining room

(Opposite Top) View of kitchen toward fireplace

(Opposite Bottom) View of kitchen volume sliding
into corridor

(Top) View of living room and porch beyond
from balcony

(Opposite) View of front entrance at night

Acknowledgments

Special thanks to:

Jim and Kathryn Polmanteer, Greg and Miki King, Myers Printing, The Film Lab,
Cindy Hutchison (special support), Dick Jackson, Ron Vance, Lee and Ann Irwin,
Rick and Samantha Shepherd, Dave and Kim Meier, Johanna and Bill Rice,
Mark Coughlin, Jeannie Taylor, Doug Ware, Lisa Vallaincourt, Noel Inocencio and
the following construction people: Dave Lewis, Doug Sherwood, Stan Mattox,
Paul Haddix, Mike Sparkman, Gary Jennings, Tony Brown, Mark Wilds, Rick Rushing
(landscape for Irwin residence), Tony Barrett (landscape for Jackson-Vance residence),
Michael W. Higdon, and Jeff Egelston. Also thanks to Len Wujcik at Alteriors.